The Big Book of
AIRPLANES

Penguin
Random
House

REVISED EDITION
Assistant editor Debangana Banerjee
Editor Ishani Nandi
US editor Margaret Parrish
Art editor Shipra Jain
Senior editors Marie Greenwood, Shatarupa Chaudhuri
Senior art editors Jim Green, Nishesh Batnagar
DTP designers Bimlesh Tiwary, Syed Md Farhan
Managing editors Laura Gilbert, Alka Thakur Hazarika
Managing art editors Diane Peyton Jones, Romi Chakraborty
CTS manager Balwant Singh
Production manager Pankaj Sharma
Producer, pre-production Nadine King
Picture researcher Aditya Katyal
Publisher Sarah Larter
Jacket designers Kartik Gera, Dheeraj Arora
Additional text Reg Grant
Consultant Reg Grant

ORIGINAL EDITION
Written and edited by Lorrie Mack
Designed by Cheryl Telfer, Helen Chapman
Publishing manager Sue Leonard
Managing art editor Clare Shedden
Jacket design Chris Drew
Picture researcher Sarah Stewart-Richardson
Production Shivani Pandey
DTP designer Almudena Díaz
DTP assistant Pilar Morales
Consultant Ben Morgan

First American Edition, 2004
This edition published in the United States in 2016 by
DK Publishing, 345 Hudson Street, New York, New York 10014

Copyright © 2004, © 2016 Dorling Kindersley Limited
DK, a Penguin Random House Company LLC
16 17 18 19 20 10 9 8 7 6 5 4 3 2
002–284735–Mar/2016

A catalog record for this book is available from the Library of Congress.

ISBN 978-1-4654-4507-0

Printed and bound in China

A WORLD OF IDEAS:
SEE ALL THERE IS TO KNOW

www.dk.com

Dorling Kindersley would like to thank: Kristin Snow at Air Tractor, Inc., Olney, Texas; Jack Brown's Seaplane Base, Florida; Dan Sweet at Columbia Helicopters, Portland, Oregon; Major Mike Chapa and John Haire at Edwards Air Force base, California; Fantasy of Flight, Florida; Chris Finnigan, BMAA, Oxfordshire; Ellen Bendell at Lockheed Martin, Palmdale, California; Beth Hagenauer at NASA Dryden Flight Research Center, Edwards, California; Nancy Machado and Duane Swing at Velocity Inc, Sebastian, Florida. The publisher would like to thank the following for their kind permission to reproduce their photographs:
Position key: c=center; b=bottom; l=left; r=right; t=top.
3 **Alamy Images**: Stocktrek Images, Inc. / Andrew Chittock (crb). **Corbis**: Transtock / Robert Kerian (cr). 4 **Donald Browning**: (tl). 6 **NASA**: (tl). 8 **NASA**: (cla). 8-9 **Deutsche Lufthansa AG**. 9 **Getty Images**: AFP / Mark RALSTON (tl); Bloomberg / Chris Ratcliffe (cr).

10 **Air Tractor Inc**: (clb). 12-13 **Velocity Inc**: (All images on the spread). 14 **E.J. Koningsveld**: (tl). **Plane Picture Company**: John M. Dibbs (c). 14-15 **E.J. Koningsveld**: (b). 15 **The Flight Collection**: Quadrant Picture Library / Chris Bennett (br). **Plane Picture Company**: John M. Dibbs (t). 16 **NASA**: Jim Ross (tl). 17 **NASA**: Tony Landis (cr). 18 **P&M Aviation**: (tl). 20 **Alamy Images**: TRISTAR PHOTOS (cl). 20-21 **Alamy Images**: i car (b); Chris Laurens (c). 21 **Alamy Images**: Peter Titmuss (tc). 22-23 **Alamy Images**: MERVYN REES (b). 22 **NASA**: (cla). 24 **Columbia Helicopters**: (tl). 26 **Edwards Airforce Base**: (bl). 42-43 **Alamy Images**: age fotostock (t). 30 **Alamy Images**: Stocktrek Images, Inc. (bl). **SpaceX**: (tr). 30-31 **SpaceX**: (c). 31 **SpaceX**: (tr).
All other images © Dorling Kindersley
For further information see: www.dkimages.com

Contents

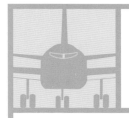
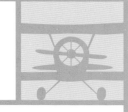

Gee Bee

Take a massive engine, add a pair of unusually short wings, and allow a tiny space for the pilot's cockpit. The result will probably look something like the spectacular Gee Bee Super Sportster, a plane that thrilled air-show crowds in 1930s US with its extraordinary speed and daredevil antics.

This *Gee Bee* has reached a top speed of 190 mph (305 kph).

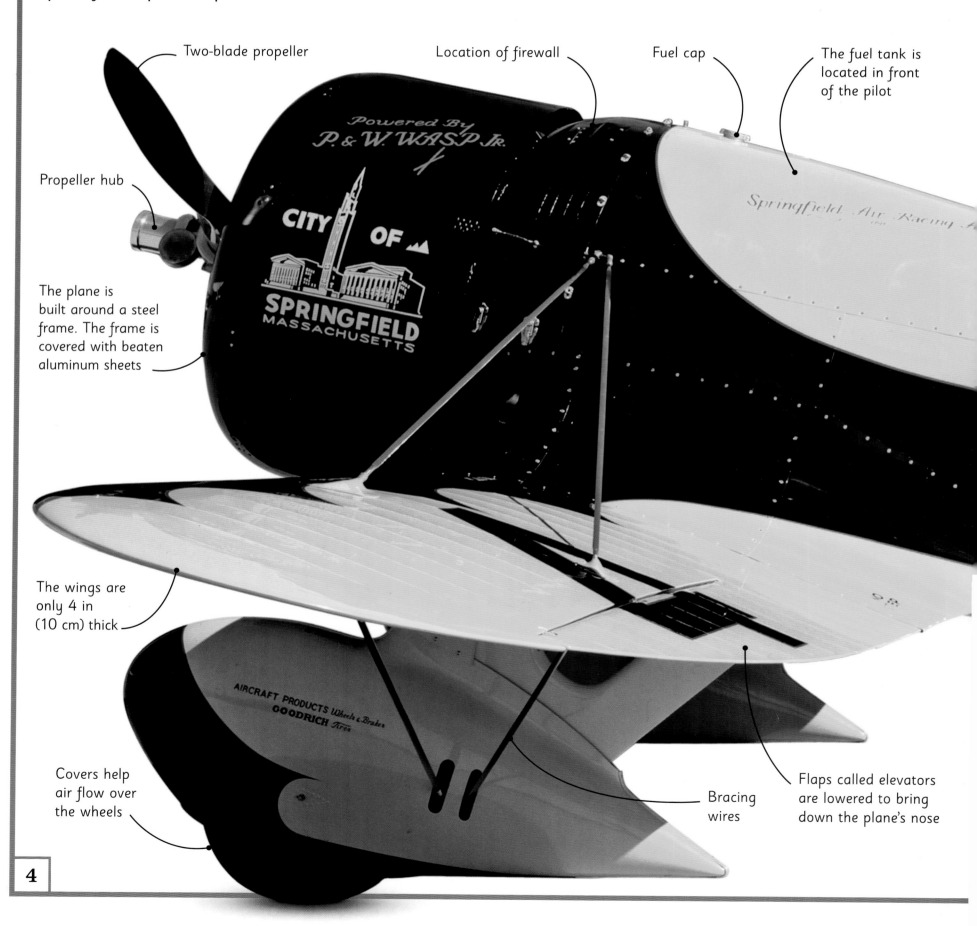

Two-blade propeller

Location of firewall

Fuel cap

The fuel tank is located in front of the pilot

Propeller hub

The plane is built around a steel frame. The frame is covered with beaten aluminum sheets

The wings are only 4 in (10 cm) thick

Covers help air flow over the wheels

Bracing wires

Flaps called elevators are lowered to bring down the plane's nose

The wingspan is around 23 ft (7 m)

Starboard or right-hand landing gear

Port or left-hand landing gear

Small but powerful

The Gee Bee is powered by a massive 535-horsepower engine. That's more than three times the power of engines commonly used in light aircraft today.

Bracing wires add strength

Pitot tube indicates air speed

Elevator

Rear landing gear, or tailwheel

Re-creating the past

The yellow-and-black Gee Bee is a replica of a 1931 plane that only flew for 124 days before crashing. The replica took two people three years to build, between 1993 and 1996.

The canopy lifts off so the pilot can climb in

The Gee Bee is just over 15 ft (4.5 m) in length

"Gee Bee" stands for Granville Brothers

NR77V

Gee Bee
SUPER SPORTSTER

Manufactured By
Granville Bros. Aircraft
INC.
Springfield Airport
Springfield, Mass.

A slice of history

The Gee Bee planes were designed to fit an airframe that was as small as possible around the largest possible engine. They took their name from the initial letters of their original inventors, the Granville Brothers. The brothers' aircraft company built a total of 23 airplanes, including three Super Sportsters.

The rudder is controlled by wire

The rudder is used to control direction

The tailwheel swivels but cannot be steered

Experimental planes

In the 1940s, the speed of sound was seen as a huge invisible barrier to the speed at which an airplane could fly. Planes that flew too near to this speed broke up after terrible buffeting. This changed with the X-planes, an experimental series of aircraft built to break all previous speed and altitude records.

The X-1E and X-15 were launched from the wing of a larger plane.

A black dart

The X-15 is an incredible plane. Only three X-15s were ever built. They made a total of 199 flights between 1959 and 1968. The fastest recorded speed was an astounding 4,522 mph (7,278 kph). It is the fastest rocket plane ever.

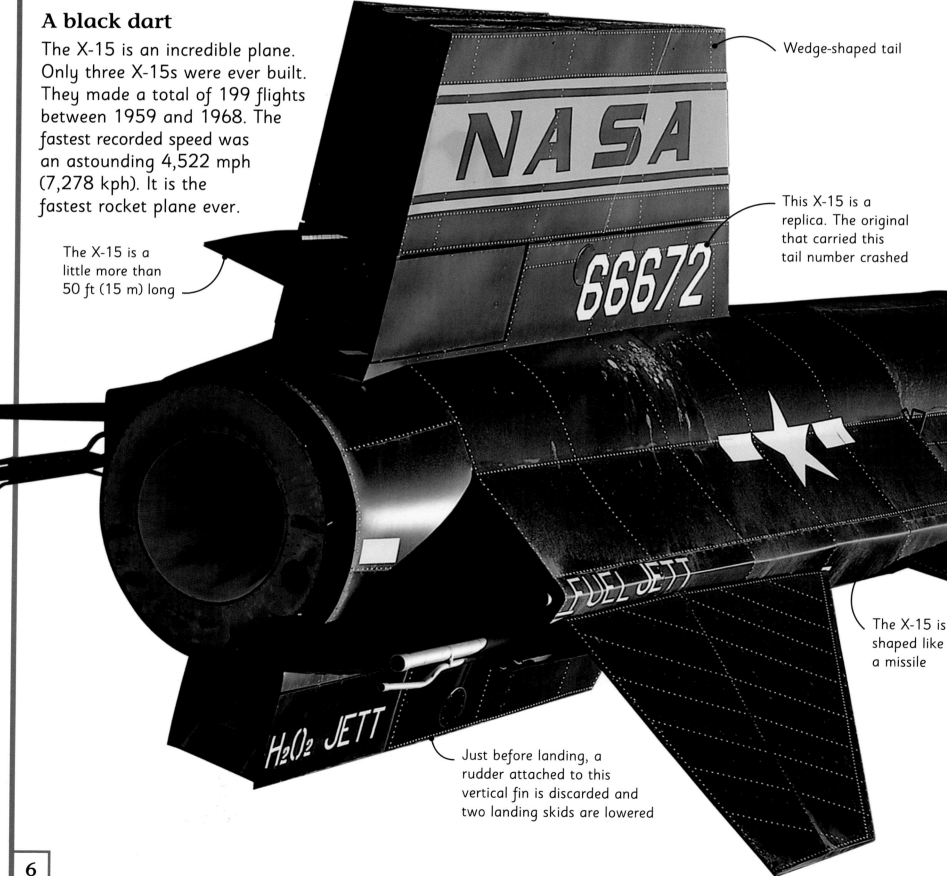

The X-15 is a little more than 50 ft (15 m) long

Wedge-shaped tail

This X-15 is a replica. The original that carried this tail number crashed

The X-15 is shaped like a missile

Just before landing, a rudder attached to this vertical fin is discarded and two landing skids are lowered

Faster than a bullet?

This plane, the X-1E, is an adapted version of the X-1, the first plane to break the sound barrier. The X-1 planes were deliberately shaped to resemble bullets. As the X-1, this plane first flew in 1946; it was modified and renamed the X-1E in 1955.

The "X" stands for experimental

The X-1E is 10 ft (3 m) high and 31 ft (9.4 m) long

In flight, the landing gear is contained beneath landing gear doors under the wings

More than half the plane's weight is taken up by fuel

There are 343 gauges in the wings that measure the different effects of speed

The high-speed wing is only $3\frac{3}{8}$ in (8.5 cm) thick

Four-chambered rocket engine

X-1E

The speed of sound varies depending on altitude. The X-1E reached a speed of 1,471 mph (2,367 kph) at an altitude of 73,458 ft (22,390 m)—more than twice the speed of sound at that height.

There is only room for one pilot

A special metal skin withstood the high temperatures of hypersonic flight

A massive rocket engine pushed the plane to travel 6,000 ft (1,829 m) per second

On one flight, the X-15 reached an altitude of 67 miles (108 km)—the first manned flight into space!

The wings are short and stubby

X-15

The rocket engine was only used for the first 80–120 seconds of the X-15's flight. The rest of the flight was completed without power.

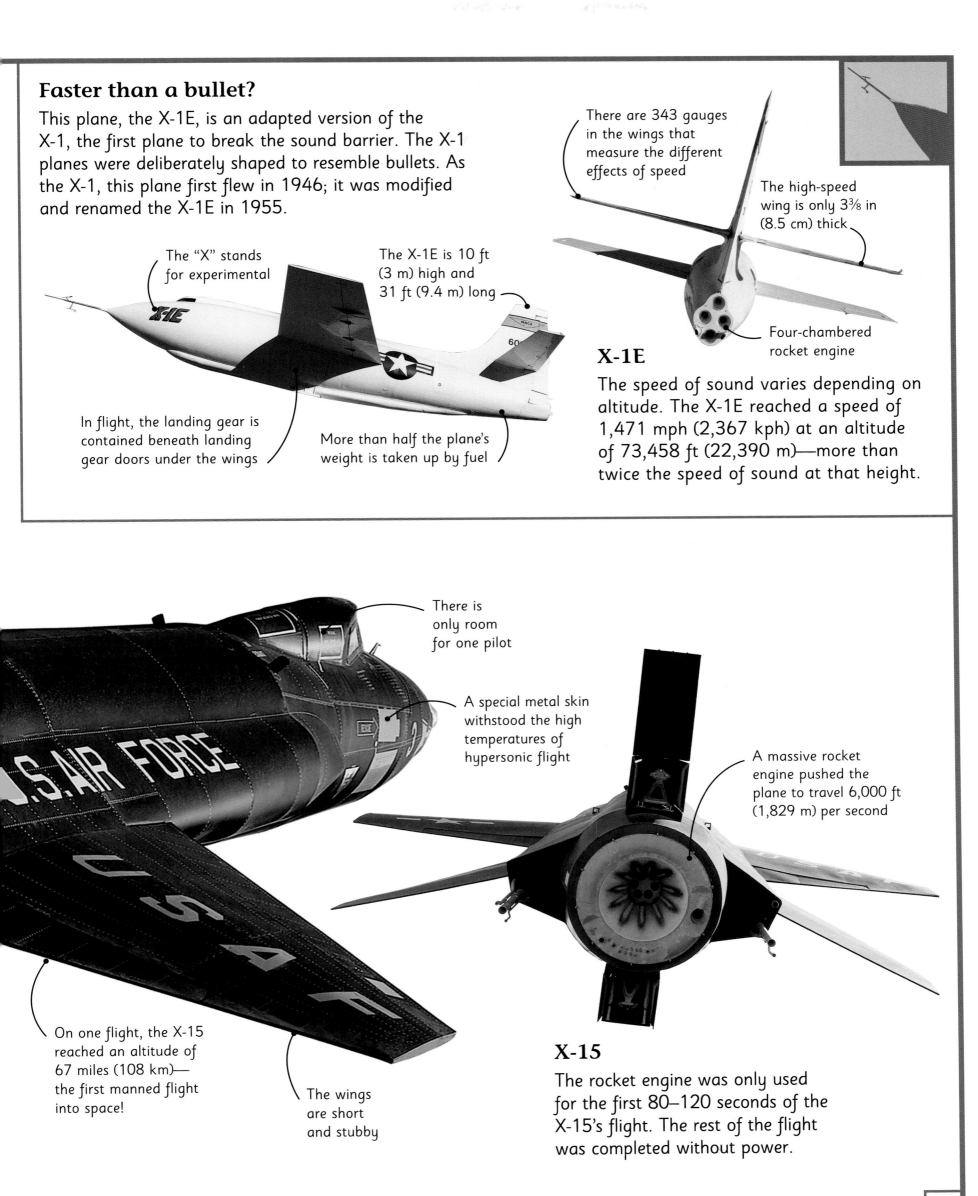

Jumbo jet

The Boeing 747, also known as the jumbo jet, was the first wide-bodied aircraft ever produced. After its introduction in 1970, it doubled the number of passengers that could be taken on one airplane. Most jumbos seat 420 passengers, but some have an internal layout that allows them to carry 660 passengers!

The tailfin is 64 ft (19.4 m) high; as high as a six-story building

Just like a car, a plane needs windshield wipers

Multipurpose plane

The jumbo jet has been modified to perform a number of different tasks. Earlier, two jumbos were adapted to ferry the American space shuttle to and from its launch site. They were strengthened to have large struts to support the shuttle.

Talking big

The jumbo jet has a massive wingspan—more than 196 ft (60 m) wide. It has a wide body with space for two aisles. The passengers may be on board for 11 hours, so the plane will be loaded with more than 800 meals and about 30 gallons (120 liters) of juice and water. Everything about the plane is big!

A wing's upper surface is curved more than its lower surface. As the engines push the plane forward, air rushing over the wings creates lift

The nose contains radar, which warns of obstacles around the aircraft—such as other planes, or an approaching storm

Each engine is covered with a protective cowling

An adult could stand up in each engine's air intake

A jumbo jet's landing gear is tested to support double the weight of the jet

The nose landing gear weighs more than a family-sized car

Upper passenger deck

Rudder

Passenger door

Baggage holds are located in the bottom of the fuselage

A small engine in the tail powers the jumbo's electrical and air-conditioning systems when on the ground

Toilet waste is stored in large tanks in the belly of the fuselage

There are 18 wheels, each 4 ft (1.25 m) in diameter

Going the distance

A jumbo jet can travel a third of the way around the world without having to stop and refuel. It carries more than 54,000 gallons (200,000 liters) of fuel in seven tanks—three located in each wing and one in the center section.

Exterior paint adds about 595 lbs (270 kg) to the weight of a jumbo jet

From bolts to wheels, there are about six million parts in a jumbo jet

Tail plane

The pilot and copilot sit on the flight deck surrounded by controls. There are even switches above their heads.

The fuselage wall is 7½ in (19 cm) thick and includes a layer of sound and heat insulation

Fuel is carried in the wings and in a center section between the wings

Landing light

The four engines are attached to the lower side of the wings

A fan draws air into each turbofan engine

Each of the four main landing gear mechanisms, or bogies, has four wheels

9

Agricultural airplane

Some farmers spray their crops to prevent damage from pests or to fertilize the crops to help them grow. They may be growing corn, peanuts, or cotton. Using an airplane is faster than using a tractor—a plane will swoop low over a field and spray a crop in minutes.

The white tip creates a white ring when the propeller spins, making it easier to see

The plane's single 750-horsepower engine is located behind the propeller

Engine exhaust

An unusual feature of this plane is that the propeller can be used to reverse the plane while taxiing on the ground

The propeller makes 2,000 revolutions (turns) each minute

Each wing is almost 6½ ft (2 m) wide

Fuel is carried in the wings

Air intake for engine

Metal struts, known as boom hangars, support the spray boom

Air leaving the wings creates a downwash that forces the spray to cover both the top and the bottom of the crop's leaves.

The landing gear is fixed and doesn't retract during flight

The pump that feeds the liquid product to the boom is turned by air flowing into this propeller

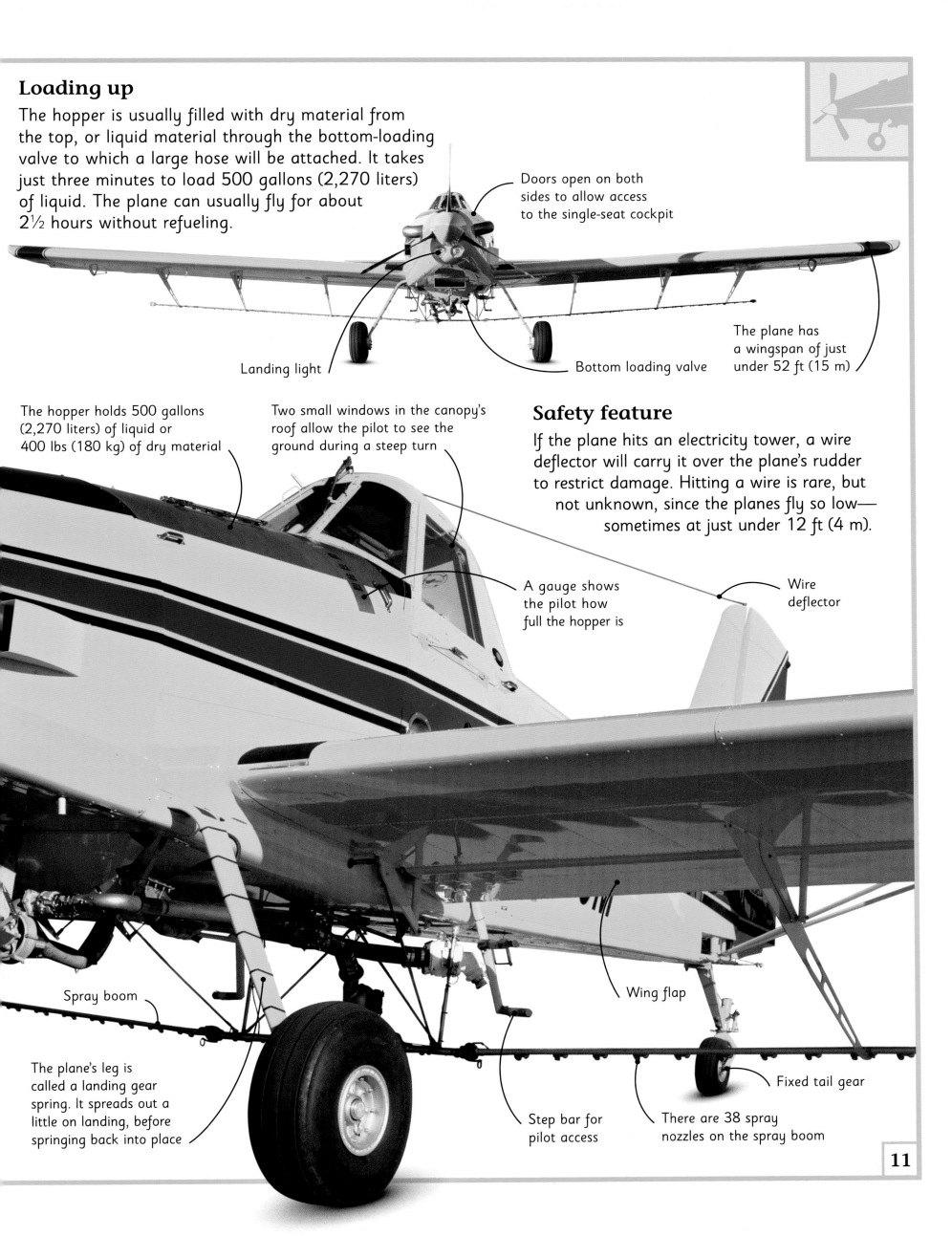

Loading up

The hopper is usually filled with dry material from the top, or liquid material through the bottom-loading valve to which a large hose will be attached. It takes just three minutes to load 500 gallons (2,270 liters) of liquid. The plane can usually fly for about 2½ hours without refueling.

Doors open on both sides to allow access to the single-seat cockpit

Landing light

Bottom loading valve

The plane has a wingspan of just under 52 ft (15 m)

The hopper holds 500 gallons (2,270 liters) of liquid or 400 lbs (180 kg) of dry material

Two small windows in the canopy's roof allow the pilot to see the ground during a steep turn

Safety feature

If the plane hits an electricity tower, a wire deflector will carry it over the plane's rudder to restrict damage. Hitting a wire is rare, but not unknown, since the planes fly so low—sometimes at just under 12 ft (4 m).

A gauge shows the pilot how full the hopper is

Wire deflector

Spray boom

The plane's leg is called a landing gear spring. It spreads out a little on landing, before springing back into place

Step bar for pilot access

Wing flap

Fixed tail gear

There are 38 spray nozzles on the spray boom

Kit airplane

Imagine buying a kit and building your own airplane in a large garage! You could put together a plane like the Velocity, an eye-catching four-seater that looks very different from most light aircraft in the skies today.

The winglet helps lift the aircraft and acts as a vertical stabilizer

The build-a-plane kits come with all the necessary nuts, bolts, and screws

Tires

The single gull-wing door opens upward

The plane seats four people, including the pilot. It can carry 600 lbs (272 kg) in weight of passengers and luggage

One big jigsaw puzzle

This Velocity kit takes about 1,200 hours to build. That's the same as working a five-day week for 34 weeks.

Pitot tube

The fiberglass body is so light that an adult can lift the nose off the ground

Small wings at the front, called canards, help to lift the aircraft

Step to aid access to cabin

In flight, the Velocity can cruise along at about 200 mph (320 kph)

Nose wheel

Why is it white?

Under the fiberglass surface is a lightweight core material that shrinks in excessive heat. A white surface doesn't absorb as much heat as a dark surface, which means that the core material is not as likely to get so hot that it shrinks.

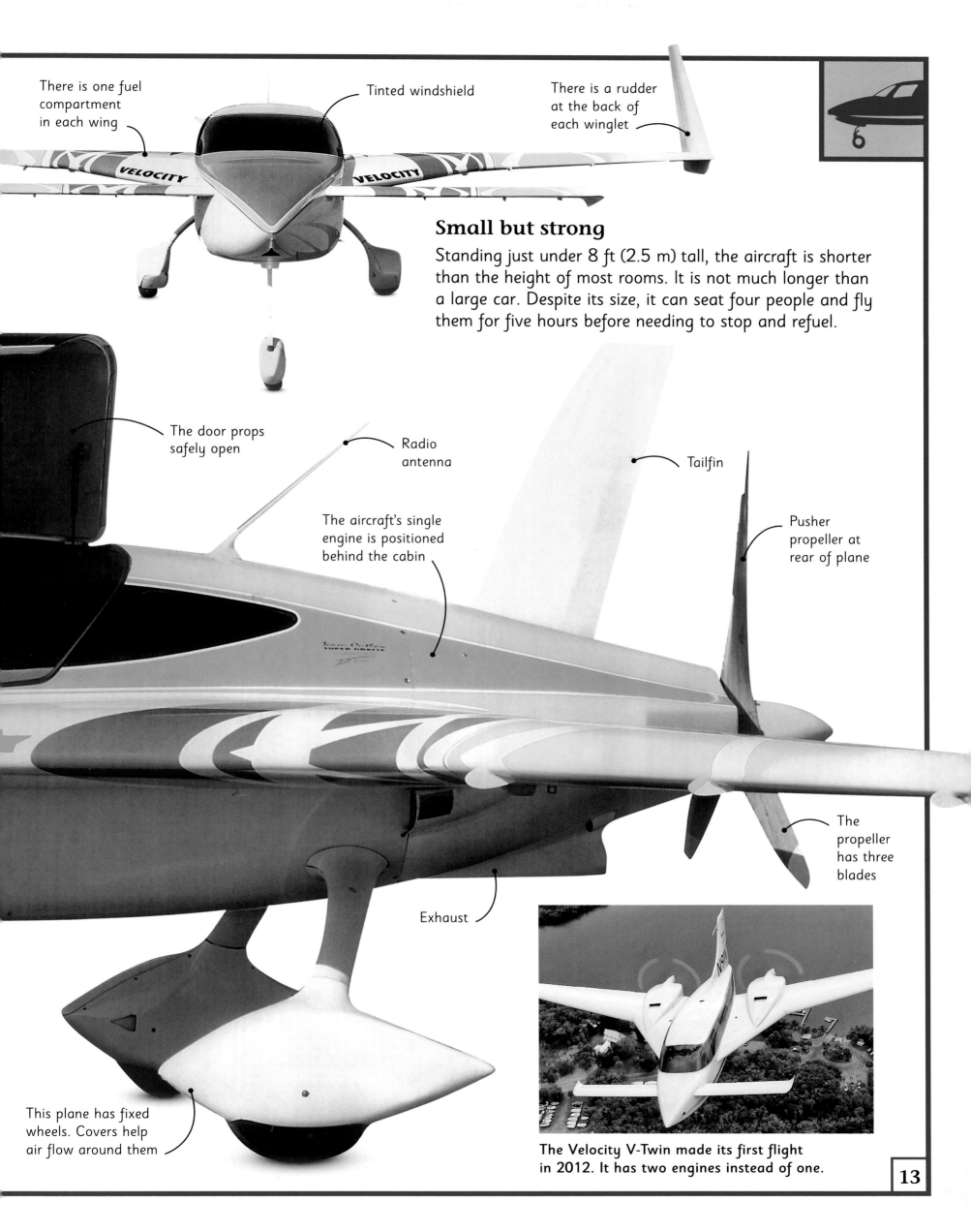

There is one fuel compartment in each wing

Tinted windshield

There is a rudder at the back of each winglet

Small but strong

Standing just under 8 ft (2.5 m) tall, the aircraft is shorter than the height of most rooms. It is not much longer than a large car. Despite its size, it can seat four people and fly them for five hours before needing to stop and refuel.

The door props safely open

Radio antenna

Tailfin

The aircraft's single engine is positioned behind the cabin

Pusher propeller at rear of plane

Exhaust

The propeller has three blades

This plane has fixed wheels. Covers help air flow around them

The Velocity V-Twin made its first flight in 2012. It has two engines instead of one.

Stunt planes

Go to an air show and you'll see brightly colored planes zipping past, wing tips almost touching. Watch as highly trained pilots take the planes into intricate loops, rolls, and flips. It's an exciting sight, with the stunt planes performing incredible air acrobatics.

One of the Red Arrows' most famous maneuvers is the Diamond Nine formation—a perfect diamond shape.

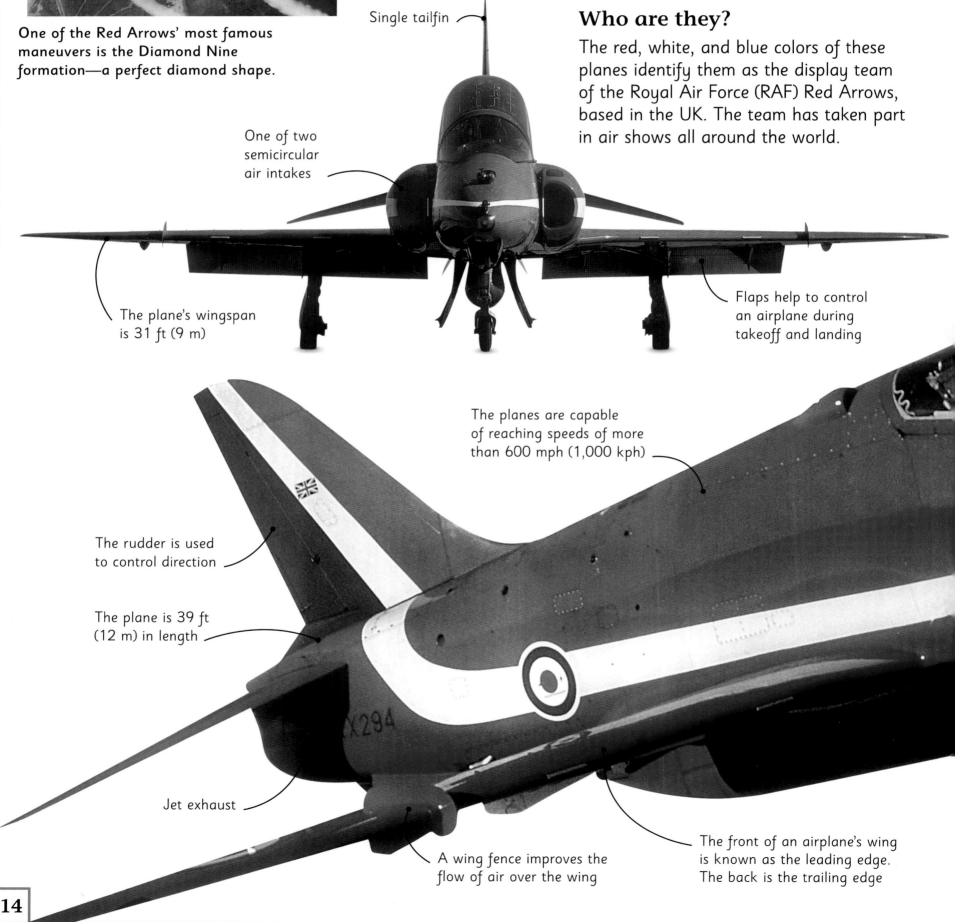

Single tailfin

One of two semicircular air intakes

The plane's wingspan is 31 ft (9 m)

Who are they?

The red, white, and blue colors of these planes identify them as the display team of the Royal Air Force (RAF) Red Arrows, based in the UK. The team has taken part in air shows all around the world.

Flaps help to control an airplane during takeoff and landing

The planes are capable of reaching speeds of more than 600 mph (1,000 kph)

The rudder is used to control direction

The plane is 39 ft (12 m) in length

Jet exhaust

A wing fence improves the flow of air over the wing

The front of an airplane's wing is known as the leading edge. The back is the trailing edge

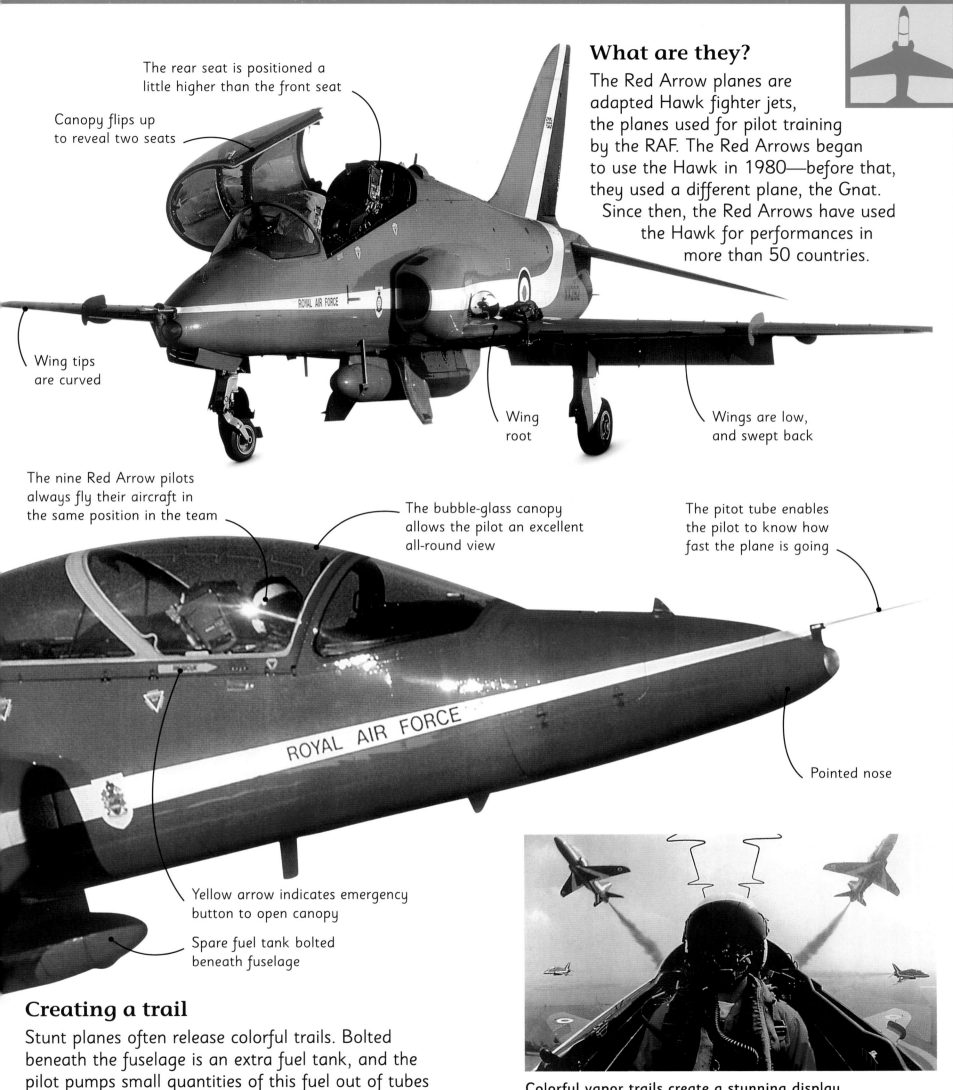

The rear seat is positioned a little higher than the front seat

Canopy flips up to reveal two seats

What are they?

The Red Arrow planes are adapted Hawk fighter jets, the planes used for pilot training by the RAF. The Red Arrows began to use the Hawk in 1980—before that, they used a different plane, the Gnat. Since then, the Red Arrows have used the Hawk for performances in more than 50 countries.

ROYAL AIR FORCE

Wing tips are curved

Wing root

Wings are low, and swept back

The nine Red Arrow pilots always fly their aircraft in the same position in the team

The bubble-glass canopy allows the pilot an excellent all-round view

The pitot tube enables the pilot to know how fast the plane is going

ROYAL AIR FORCE

Pointed nose

Yellow arrow indicates emergency button to open canopy

Spare fuel tank bolted beneath fuselage

Creating a trail

Stunt planes often release colorful trails. Bolted beneath the fuselage is an extra fuel tank, and the pilot pumps small quantities of this fuel out of tubes above the jet exhaust. The heat here vaporizes the fuel, and it is mixed with red or blue dye to create a trail.

Colorful vapor trails create a stunning display as the pilots take their planes through the different maneuvers of an air show.

Flying laboratory

This unusual-looking, long-nosed plane is designed to cruise at altitudes of around 13.5 miles (22 km). That's more than twice the cruising altitude of a jumbo jet! It needs to do this because it is a flying science aircraft, or flying laboratory, specially equipped to collect information about the Earth. Its official name is the ER-2.

The ER-2 has four compartments that hold experiments. One is in the fuselage, one is in the nose, and two are in pods that can be attached to the wings.

A typical mission

After takeoff, the ER-2 will reach its cruising altitude in around 20 minutes. The plane can travel more than 3,000 miles (4,800 km) each time it goes on a mission, although typical missions are shorter. It will usually be up for around six hours.

Cockpit canopy tips upward to open

There is room for one pilot who sits in an ejection seat

Rearview mirror

The top of the nose cone is covered with an antiglare material. This helps to keep reflected light out of the pilot's eyes

The antenna receives satellite signals, which are used to calculate the aircraft's position and speed

Top of support wheel, or pogo

An external rescue button opens the canopy

Different nose cones can be attached, depending on the experiment

The pitot tube calculates air speed and altitude

What does it do?

The ER-2 monitors changes in the weather, the sea, and geography of the Earth. It can be used to test the behavior of new technology under extreme conditions.

The ER-2 is operated by NASA (National Aeronautics and Space Administration)

Most fuel is carried in the wings

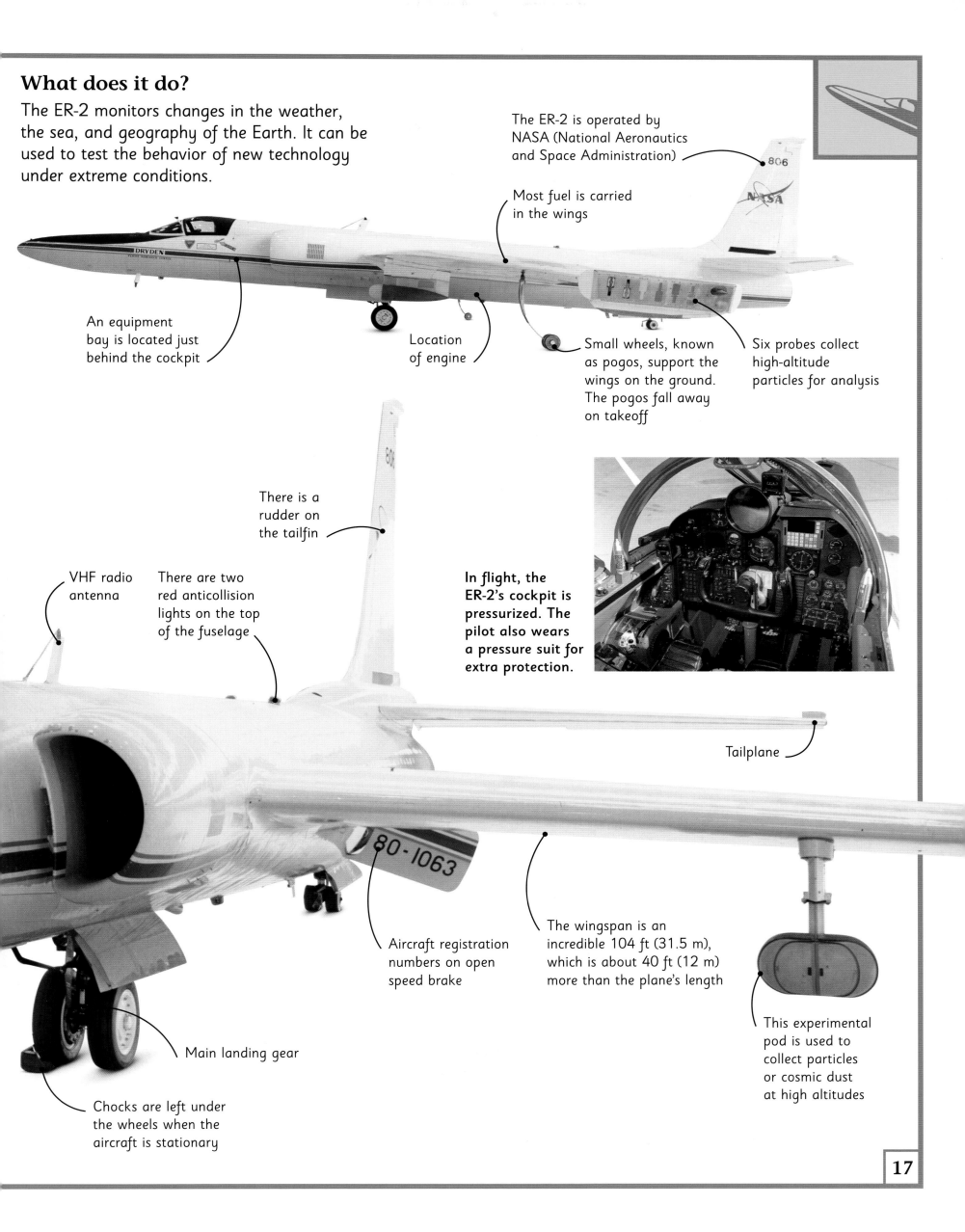

An equipment bay is located just behind the cockpit

Location of engine

Small wheels, known as pogos, support the wings on the ground. The pogos fall away on takeoff

Six probes collect high-altitude particles for analysis

There is a rudder on the tailfin

VHF radio antenna

There are two red anticollision lights on the top of the fuselage

In flight, the ER-2's cockpit is pressurized. The pilot also wears a pressure suit for extra protection.

Tailplane

80-1063

Aircraft registration numbers on open speed brake

The wingspan is an incredible 104 ft (31.5 m), which is about 40 ft (12 m) more than the plane's length

Main landing gear

Chocks are left under the wheels when the aircraft is stationary

This experimental pod is used to collect particles or cosmic dust at high altitudes

Microlight

Although it looks small, this microlight can stay in the air for up to four hours, burning up fuel at the rate of 3 gallons (12 liters) per hour. Many microlight pilots take part in competitions, performing a series of tasks such as photographing things on the ground, or switching off the engine before landing. It is an exciting sport.

Microlights usually fly at about 3,000 ft (900 m)—a jumbo jet flies at 10 times that height.

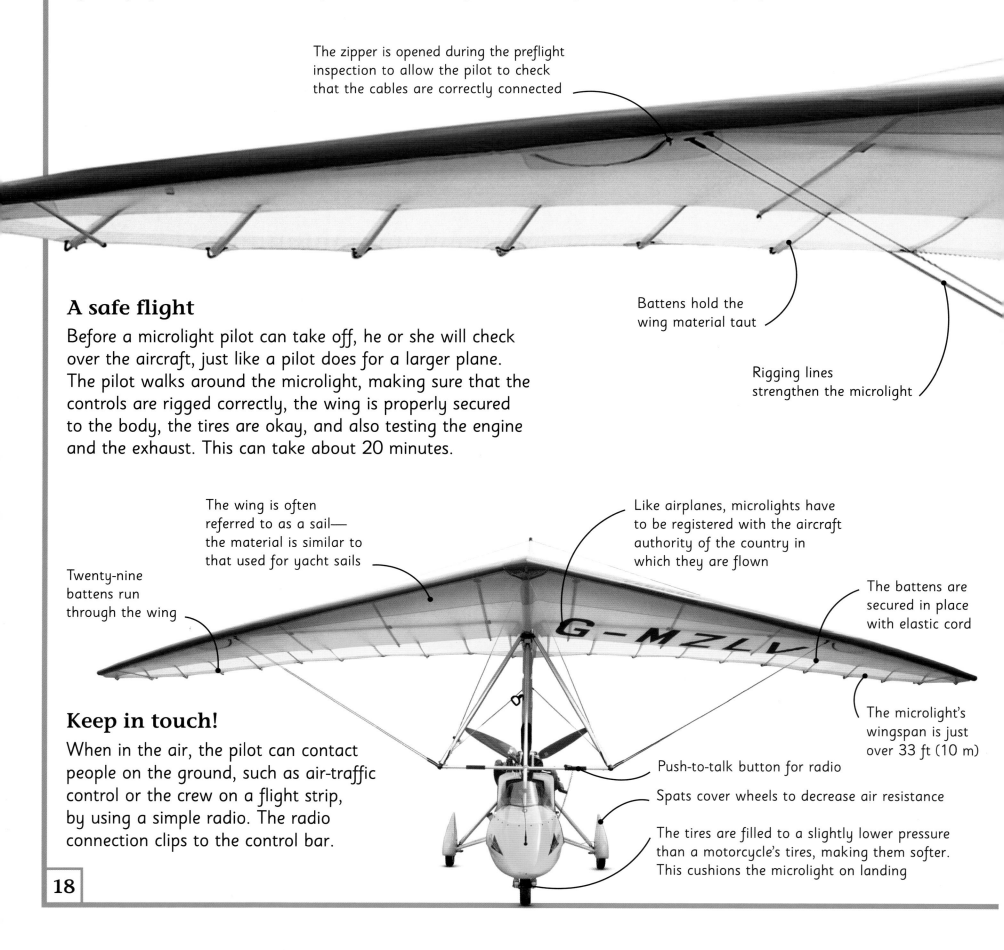

The zipper is opened during the preflight inspection to allow the pilot to check that the cables are correctly connected

Battens hold the wing material taut

Rigging lines strengthen the microlight

A safe flight

Before a microlight pilot can take off, he or she will check over the aircraft, just like a pilot does for a larger plane. The pilot walks around the microlight, making sure that the controls are rigged correctly, the wing is properly secured to the body, the tires are okay, and also testing the engine and the exhaust. This can take about 20 minutes.

The wing is often referred to as a sail—the material is similar to that used for yacht sails

Like airplanes, microlights have to be registered with the aircraft authority of the country in which they are flown

Twenty-nine battens run through the wing

The battens are secured in place with elastic cord

The microlight's wingspan is just over 33 ft (10 m)

Keep in touch!

When in the air, the pilot can contact people on the ground, such as air-traffic control or the crew on a flight strip, by using a simple radio. The radio connection clips to the control bar.

G-MZLV

Push-to-talk button for radio

Spats cover wheels to decrease air resistance

The tires are filled to a slightly lower pressure than a motorcycle's tires, making them softer. This cushions the microlight on landing

18

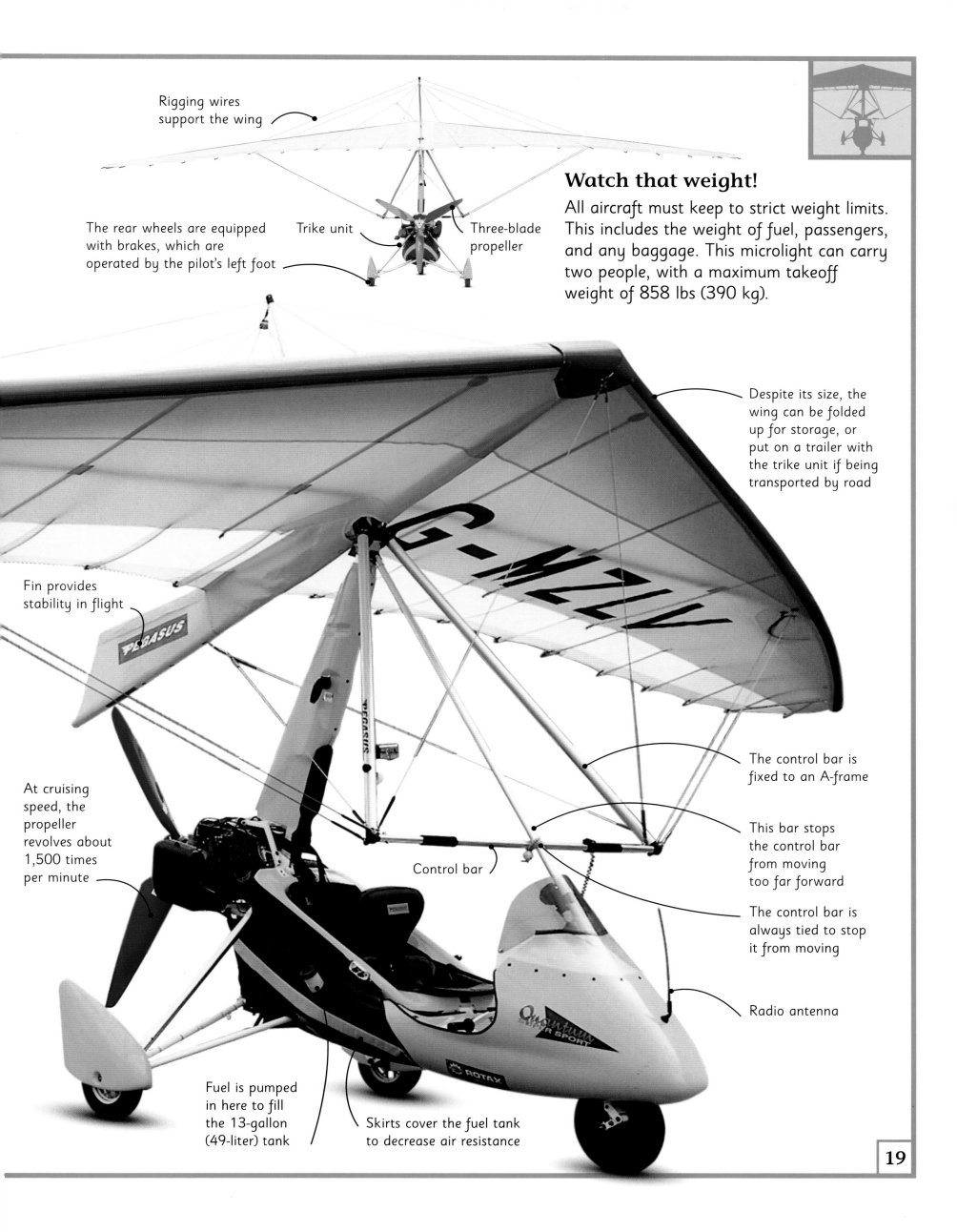

Rigging wires support the wing

Trike unit

Three-blade propeller

The rear wheels are equipped with brakes, which are operated by the pilot's left foot

Watch that weight!

All aircraft must keep to strict weight limits. This includes the weight of fuel, passengers, and any baggage. This microlight can carry two people, with a maximum takeoff weight of 858 lbs (390 kg).

Despite its size, the wing can be folded up for storage, or put on a trailer with the trike unit if being transported by road

Fin provides stability in flight

PEGASUS

G-MZLV

At cruising speed, the propeller revolves about 1,500 times per minute

Control bar

The control bar is fixed to an A-frame

This bar stops the control bar from moving too far forward

The control bar is always tied to stop it from moving

Radio antenna

Fuel is pumped in here to fill the 13-gallon (49-liter) tank

Skirts cover the fuel tank to decrease air resistance

The Concorde

The Concorde was a supersonic airliner, capable of carrying passengers at more than twice the speed of sound. In a record flight, it crossed the Atlantic Ocean, from New York to London, in just under three hours—less than half the time a jumbo jet takes. It also cruised along at about twice the altitude of a jumbo, so its passengers could see the curve of the Earth. The Concorde was in regular service with British and French airlines from 1976 to 2003.

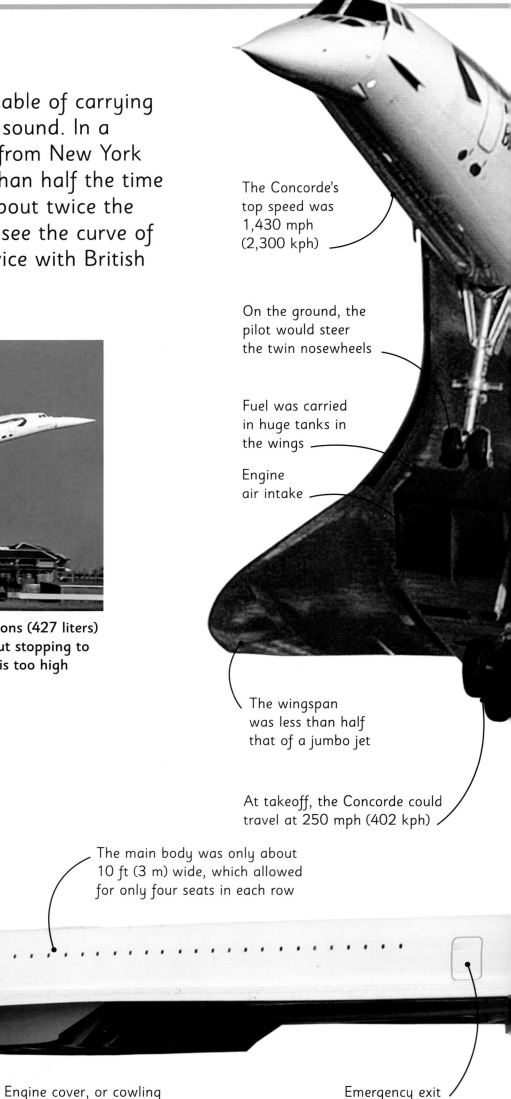

The Concorde's top speed was 1,430 mph (2,300 kph)

On the ground, the pilot would steer the twin nosewheels

Fuel was carried in huge tanks in the wings

Engine air intake

The wingspan was less than half that of a jumbo jet

At takeoff, the Concorde could travel at 250 mph (402 kph)

Once in the air, the Concorde guzzled fuel at the rate of 111 gallons (427 liters) each minute. It could travel about 3,740 miles (5,900 km) without stopping to refuel, and flew at an altitude of about 10 miles (16 km), which is too high to be affected by air turbulence.

VHF antenna

Upper rudder

Tailfin

The main body was only about 10 ft (3 m) wide, which allowed for only four seats in each row

G-BOAC

Tail cone

Rear emergency exit

Engine cover, or cowling

Emergency exit

The Concorde could carry 128 passengers, depending on the weight of cargo and fuel carried on board

Designed for speed, the triangular, swept-back wings were known as Delta wings

The wings were covered with de-icing panels to prevent a buildup of ice

The Concorde first flew in 1969, so the flight deck did not have the digital screen displays familiar to modern cockpits.

Crossing the speed of sound

When an airplane flies faster than the speed of sound, it produces a sonic boom. This is a loud noise a bit like a clap of thunder. It happens because the airplane creates waves in the air, just like a boat does in water. The boom is heard by people on the ground, but passengers on board don't hear anything.

The Concorde had four turbojet engines, two under each wing

Thrust reversers were used to help the plane slow down on landing. They changed the direction in which the engine was pushing

Four-wheel carriage, or bogie

Twin-wheel tail bumper

VHF antenna

Aerodynamic strake directed airflow around the cockpit area

Retractable visor

BRITISH AIRWAYS

The Concorde's nose could be straightened, or dropped down

A moveable nose

The Concorde's nose straightened out when the plane was flying. This helped the plane to cut through the air. It dropped down for takeoff and landing, so that the pilot had a better view of the runway. The nose contained radar equipment.

Blackbird

The Blackbird, or SR-71A, was the perfect spy plane. Not only could it fly at an amazing 2,000 mph (3,218 kph)—more than three times the speed of sound—but its onboard cameras could read a license plate on a car from 17 miles (27 km) up. The Blackbird served with the US Air Force from 1964 to 1998.

The plane expanded by 11 in (28 cm) in flight

Protective covers had to be removed before takeoff

On the way up, fuel streaked out. The plane's fuel tanks leaked until they expanded and sealed as a result of high temperatures caused by speed.

The SR-71A carried a crew of two—a pilot and a reconnaissance systems officer

In flight, the cone pulled back 26 in (66 cm) to control the air allowed into the engine

The whole rudder moved on a hinge at the base

The plane was refueled in midair through a refueling port or opening in the Blackbird's skin

A curved edge, known as a chine, provided lift and stability to the front of the aircraft

Circular air intake (protected when on the ground) supplied air to the engine

Fuel more than doubled the empty weight of the plane

Blackbird was faster than a rifle bullet

Landing lights

Front landing gear

Smash those records!

The Blackbird remains the fastest jet-engine aircraft ever built. It set a number of world speed records in 1976, reaching 2,193 mph (3,530 kph). It also set an altitude record for a jet-engine aircraft of 85,069 ft (25,930 m).

Don't touch!

By the time it landed, the Blackbird's body became too hot to touch for about an hour. The pilot had to step clear on special steps that were wheeled up to the plane. Parts of the plane's body reached the same temperature as that of a hot oven.

Red lines marked the limits of where ground mechanics could step

There were ejection seats in case of emergency

One of two engines

Food was carried in tubes. The crew held the tubes against the cockpit glass to warm the food!

Getting bigger

Each engine was almost 18 ft (5.5 m) in length. But it expanded another 6 in (15 cm) in flight because of the heat!

The crew had to wear protective, high altitude pressure suits, similar to the suits astronauts wear

One jet engine was contained here

In less than one hour, Blackbird could photograph an area 100,000 sq miles (259,000 sq km)

Landing gear retracted when the plane was in flight to produce a smooth, aerodynamic shape

Gear doors closed to seal in the landing gear after takeoff

When the plane climbed, the engines used up a total of about 8,000 gallons (36,370 liters) of fuel per hour

Tires were 10 times thicker than a car tire

Chinook helicopter

A helicopter can hover and pick up a load from a very restricted space. It might be lifting logs from a heavily wooded hillside or transporting huge pipes. This Chinook helicopter is unusually powerful. It has been stripped of unnecessary equipment to make it lighter so that it can lift more than its own weight in cargo. It is known as a utility Chinook.

The hefty steel cable used to lift loads is 1 in (2.5 cm) thick and 200 ft (60 m) long.

A thirst for fuel

Helicopter engines burn up a lot of fuel spinning the rotors to lift the machine up. During routine heavy-lift operations, this Chinook uses 333 gallons (1,515 liters) of fuel per hour. It is typically refueled every 1½ hours.

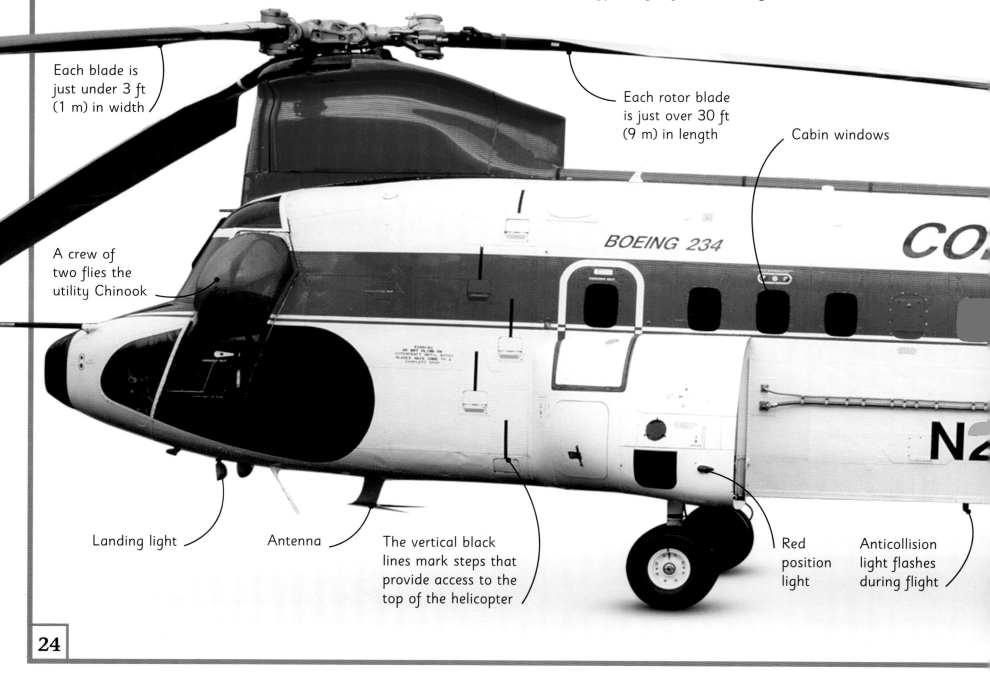

Each blade is just under 3 ft (1 m) in width

Each rotor blade is just over 30 ft (9 m) in length

Cabin windows

BOEING 234

CO

A crew of two flies the utility Chinook

N2

Landing light

Antenna

The vertical black lines mark steps that provide access to the top of the helicopter

Red position light

Anticollision light flashes during flight

Flight control

A pilot works with a copilot, so the cockpit controls are the same on both sides. Both pilot and copilot have more than 150 control buttons and switches around them.

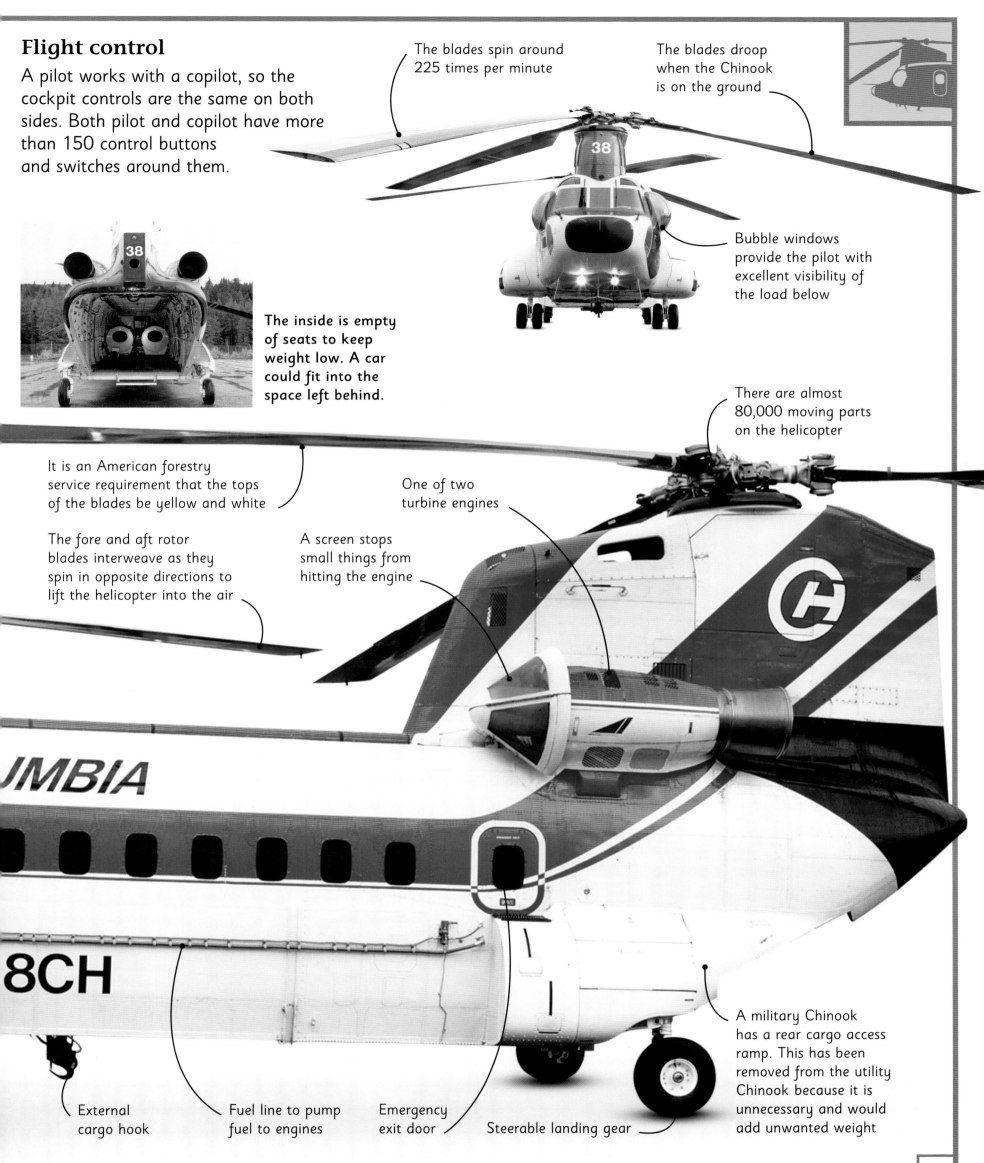

The blades spin around 225 times per minute

The blades droop when the Chinook is on the ground

Bubble windows provide the pilot with excellent visibility of the load below

The inside is empty of seats to keep weight low. A car could fit into the space left behind.

There are almost 80,000 moving parts on the helicopter

It is an American forestry service requirement that the tops of the blades be yellow and white

One of two turbine engines

The fore and aft rotor blades interweave as they spin in opposite directions to lift the helicopter into the air

A screen stops small things from hitting the engine

A military Chinook has a rear cargo access ramp. This has been removed from the utility Chinook because it is unnecessary and would add unwanted weight

External cargo hook

Fuel line to pump fuel to engines

Emergency exit door

Steerable landing gear

F-16

The F-16 is a multirole fighter aircraft, originally designed for close-up air combat. It is also used for air-to-ground attack. It has excellent maneuverability. Flying at a height of 7.5 miles (12 km), an F-16 can reach a speed of 1,350 mph (2,172 kph)—more than twice the speed of sound. The F-16 is officially known as the Fighting Falcon, but all the pilots call it the Viper.

Raised canopy

Instructor pilot

Trainee pilot

RESCUE

U.S. FORCE

Forward landing gear

This specially adapted pitot tube is only used for flight tests

Getting ready to go

The pilots and ground crew have lots of checks to complete before they are ready to take off. These take them about 45 minutes—they check everything, including the flight controls.

The cockpit is equipped with a visual display screen known as a Heads-Up-Display. It tells the pilots where they are and displays weapons and targeting information

Pitot tube

MAJ. ROB ADAM

RESCUE
1. PUSH BUTTON TO OPEN DOOR
2. PULL RING OUT 6 FEET TO JETTISON CANOPY

A bright yellow arrow points to a handle. Ground crew members pull this to pop open the canopy in an emergency

The forward landing gear retracts into a compartment in flight

The first F-16s had black radomes (or radar covers). Pilots felt it was an easy target for enemy fire, so the black was changed to gray

The F-16 is the most commonly used aircraft in the US Air Force. It is also used in many other countries.

The F-16 has a unique flight control system known as fly-by-wire. It means that computers and electronics have replaced many of the older-style mechanical workings

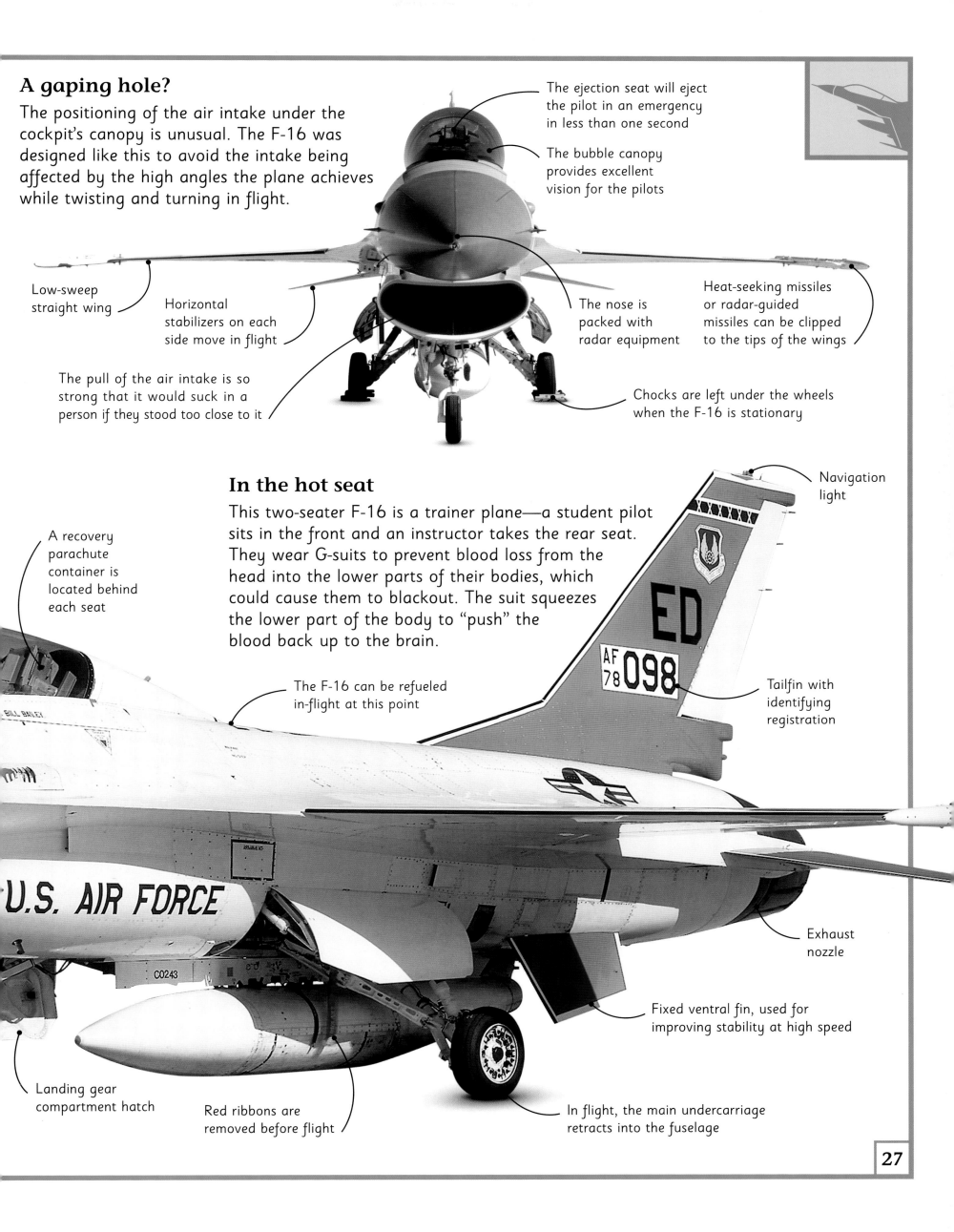

A gaping hole?

The positioning of the air intake under the cockpit's canopy is unusual. The F-16 was designed like this to avoid the intake being affected by the high angles the plane achieves while twisting and turning in flight.

The ejection seat will eject the pilot in an emergency in less than one second

The bubble canopy provides excellent vision for the pilots

Low-sweep straight wing

Horizontal stabilizers on each side move in flight

The pull of the air intake is so strong that it would suck in a person if they stood too close to it

The nose is packed with radar equipment

Heat-seeking missiles or radar-guided missiles can be clipped to the tips of the wings

Chocks are left under the wheels when the F-16 is stationary

In the hot seat

This two-seater F-16 is a trainer plane—a student pilot sits in the front and an instructor takes the rear seat. They wear G-suits to prevent blood loss from the head into the lower parts of their bodies, which could cause them to blackout. The suit squeezes the lower part of the body to "push" the blood back up to the brain.

Navigation light

A recovery parachute container is located behind each seat

The F-16 can be refueled in-flight at this point

ED

AF 78 098

Tailfin with identifying registration

BILL BAILEY

U.S. AIR FORCE

C0243

Landing gear compartment hatch

Red ribbons are removed before flight

In flight, the main undercarriage retracts into the fuselage

Exhaust nozzle

Fixed ventral fin, used for improving stability at high speed

Green starboard light

Seaplane

Seaplanes are equipped with floats instead of wheels, so they can take off or land wherever there is a flat stretch of water. They are mostly used in areas that have few airfields but plenty of lakes, rivers, or calm coastal seas.

Which side is which?

Like boats, airplanes have a red port light on the left side and a green starboard light on the right side. At night, these lights help to identify which direction the plane is facing.

There are four doors, two on each side

The pilot's controls and instrument panels are in the cockpit

Hinged flaps on the back of the wings control the seaplane's flying height

A ventral fin helps to stabilize the seaplane in flight

Small rudders at the back of the floats allow the pilot to steer the plane in the water

Rudder-control wires

Starboard, or right-hand, float

One of two spreader bars

"Step" allows for less drag in water, enabling acceleration

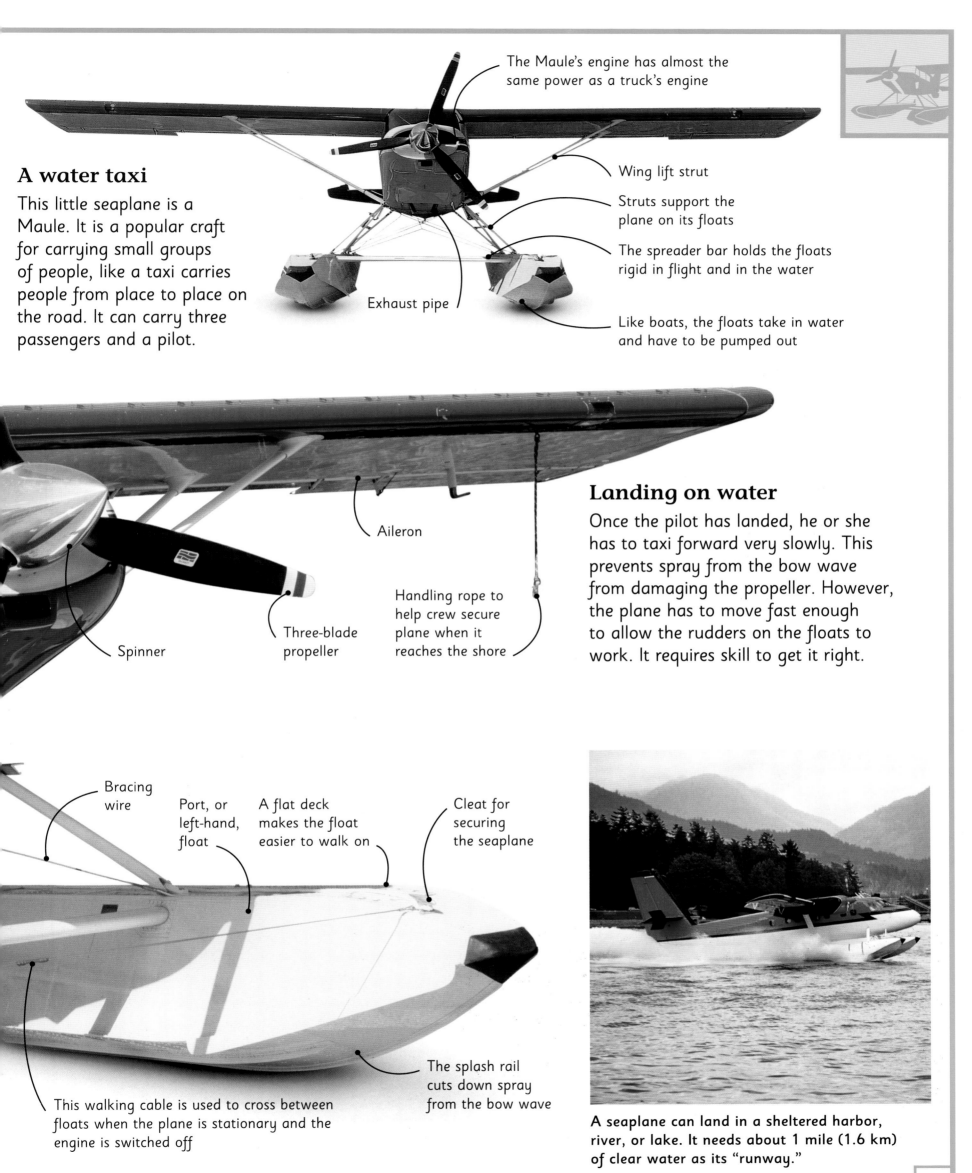

The Maule's engine has almost the same power as a truck's engine

A water taxi

This little seaplane is a Maule. It is a popular craft for carrying small groups of people, like a taxi carries people from place to place on the road. It can carry three passengers and a pilot.

Wing lift strut

Struts support the plane on its floats

The spreader bar holds the floats rigid in flight and in the water

Exhaust pipe

Like boats, the floats take in water and have to be pumped out

Aileron

Spinner

Three-blade propeller

Handling rope to help crew secure plane when it reaches the shore

Landing on water

Once the pilot has landed, he or she has to taxi forward very slowly. This prevents spray from the bow wave from damaging the propeller. However, the plane has to move fast enough to allow the rudders on the floats to work. It requires skill to get it right.

Bracing wire

Port, or left-hand, float

A flat deck makes the float easier to walk on

Cleat for securing the seaplane

The splash rail cuts down spray from the bow wave

This walking cable is used to cross between floats when the plane is stationary and the engine is switched off

A seaplane can land in a sheltered harbor, river, or lake. It needs about 1 mile (1.6 km) of clear water as its "runway."

Space flight

The first person flew into space in 1961. Since then astronauts have walked on the Moon and been on space stations that orbit the Earth, while space probes have explored the far reaches of the solar system. Today, SpaceX Dragon, a free-flying, reusable spacecraft, represents the best of cutting-edge space travel technology in the 21st century.

The Dragon spacecraft is launched into orbit atop a two-stage Falcon 9 rocket. The Falcon has a total of 10 rocket engines.

Solar cells use the Sun's rays to provide energy for onboard systems

The Dragon craft

The SpaceX Dragon is an unmanned vehicle that carries cargo to and from the International Space Station (ISS). It consists of a pressurized capsule and unpressurized trunk. The capsule is reusable. It reenters the atmosphere protected by a heat shield, and makes a soft landing on the Earth.

Trunk hold has a capacity for 490 cubic ft (14 cubic m) of cargo

Docked in space

A Dragon spacecraft first docked at the International Space Station in 2012. Docking means attaching one spacecraft with another in space. Remote-controlled thrusters move the spacecraft to docking. A robotic arm from the space station secures the Dragon while cargo is loaded and unloaded through a hatch, or small opening, in the capsule's nose.

Advanced capsule

The Dragon's pressurized capsule is fully suitable for manned flight. A manned version of the spacecraft, the Crew Dragon, is planned to act as a replacement for the Space Shuttle. It is expected to be ready to carry up to seven crew or passengers by 2018.

Cone protecting top of capsule is jettisoned after launch

Height of vehicle with its trunk is 23 ft (7 m)

Docking hatch links capsule to space station

Pressurized capsule carries cargo and, potentially, crew

Draco thrusters move the capsule

Frame supports capsule when it's out of service

Advanced PICA-X heat shield protects capsule on reentry

Solar arrays unfold from trunk in space

Unpressurized trunk carries cargo and houses solar panels

Solar panels are ditched along with the trunk before reentry

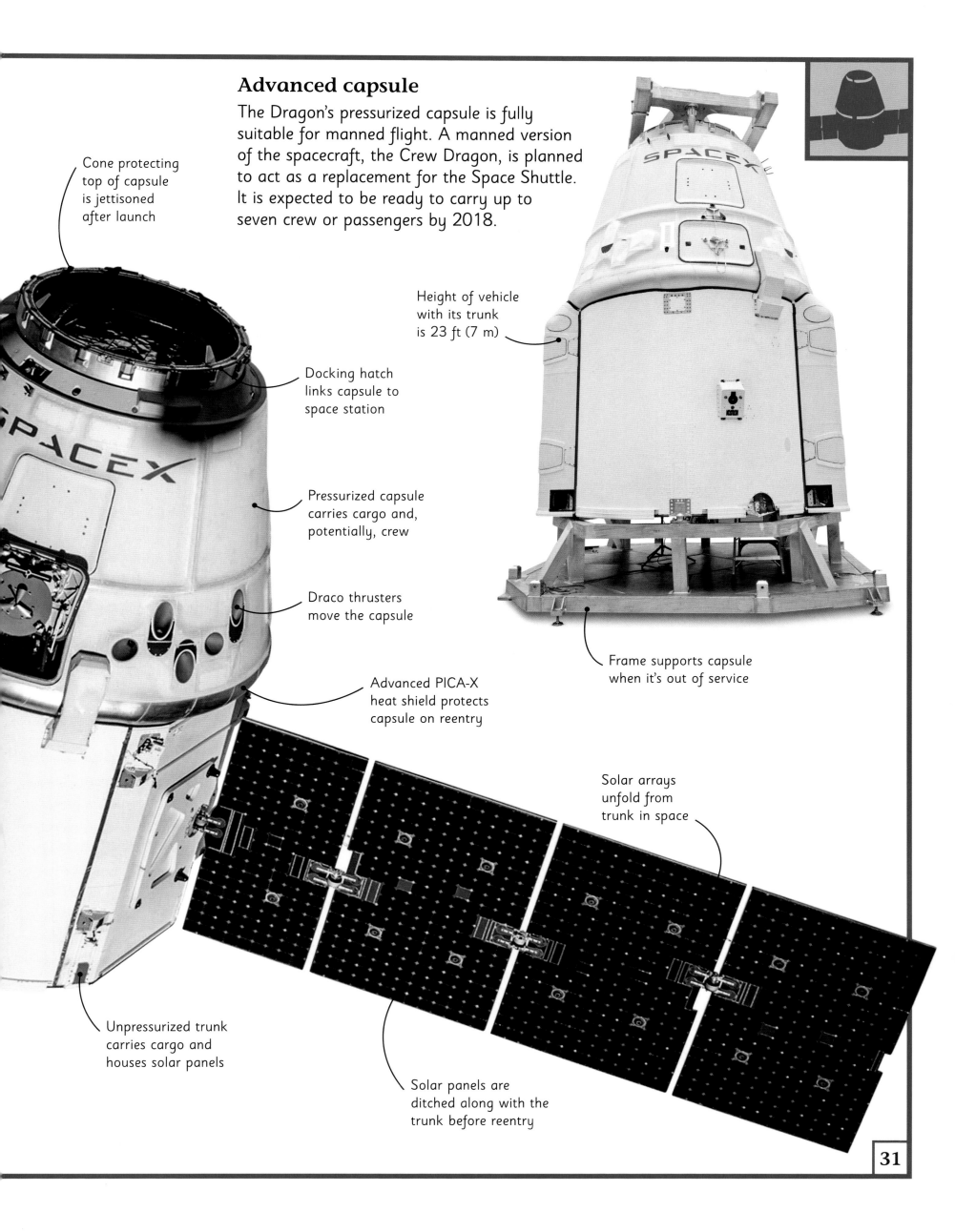

31

Glossary

aerodynamic Shape designed to cut through air smoothly and cleanly

aileron Flap close to a plane's wingtip that is used to control the rolling motion of a plane

air intake Place where air is taken into a machine. Air is needed to mix with fuel to make an engine go

altitude Height of an object above land or sea level

antenna Wire or rod that sticks out from an object to pick up radio waves

avionics Aircraft's electronic and navigation equipment

ejection seat Seat that contains an explosive charge and a parachute. It can be ejected from an airplane in an emergency to save the pilot

elevator Flat control surface that is used to make a plane climb or dive

exhaust Pipe through which waste fumes are pushed out from an engine

fuselage Body of an aircraft

horsepower Measure of an engine's power. One unit of horsepower is loosely based on the power of a horse

hypersonic Plane traveling at more than five times the speed of sound

infrared Type of radiation given off by hot objects. It is invisible to the eye, but special sensors can detect it

jet engine All engines need fuel and oxygen to make them go. A "jet" engine uses a jet of air for extra thrust

landing gear Wheels of an airplane

pitot tube Pipe that sticks out from an aircraft and measures air speed

port Left-hand side of a ship or airplane

radar Means of detecting objects that are not within sight by bouncing radio waves off them

rocket engine Type of jet engine that carries the oxygen it needs in a tank

rudder Hinged flap at the back of the plane that is used to turn an aircraft to the left or right

speed of sound Sound travels at about 760 mph (1,224 kph)

starboard Right-hand side of a ship or airplane

supersonic Aircraft that flies faster than the speed of sound

thermal protection External coating or covering that protects an airplane from too much heat

undercarriage Landing gear of an aircraft

Index